AMAZON PRIME

THE WORLD'S LEADING
SUBSCRIPTION BUSINESS

PATRICIA WILSON

Contents

1 OVERVIEW: MAIN POINTS AND CONCLUSIONS   1

2 INTRODUCTION: AMAZON PRIME – THE WORLD'S MOST SUCCESSFUL SUBSCRIPTION BUSINESS?   4

3 BEHIND PRIME   8

4 BEHIND THE SUCCESS – THE 'GOLDEN HANDCUFFS'; BENEFITS FOR SUBSCRIBERS   10

5 PRIME IN NUMBERS   13

6 THE DEVELOPMENT OF PRIME   16

6.1 FREE TWO-DAY DELIVERY	16
6.2 PRIME INSTANT VIDEO	18
6.3 AMAZON STUDIOS	19
6.4 PRIME MUSIC	20
6.5 AMAZON CLOUD DRIVE	21
6.6 AMAZON MOM	22
6.7 SIX MONTHS OF FREE MEMBERSHIP FOR STUDENTS	22

6.8 KINDLE AND PRIME LIBRARY 23
6.9 PRIME NOW 23
6.10 PRIME FREE – SAME-DAY DELIVERY 24
6.11 AMAZON PRIME AIR 25
6.12 PRIME DAY 26
6.13 AMAZON DASH BUTTON 26

7 THE LONG-TERM STRATEGY BEHIND PRIME 28

8 AMAZONFRESH AND PRIMEFRESH 30

9 CONCLUSION: WHAT CAN OTHERS LEARN FROM AMAZON? 32

10 ABOUT SUBSCRYBE 37

1 OVERVIEW: MAIN POINTS AND CONCLUSIONS

• Amazon is the world's leading e-commerce business with an annual turnover of more than 100 billion USD and its growth is still exponential. At the same time, Amazon is one of the world's leading subscription businesses with Amazon Prime.

The service is believed to have 63 million members worldwide.

• Amazon prime is considered a significant part of Amazon's great success. Amazon Prime members pay an annual sum of 99 USD or a monthly sum of 10.99 USD and get free two-day delivery on more than 15 million different items. Furthermore, Amazon provides its Prime members with different content including data storage, movies and music.

• The primary purpose for Amazon Prime is to create loyalty between Amazon and its customers.

When the customer has paid 99 or 10.99 USD for free delivery he or she will automatically wish to get most out of the already paid subscription fee.

In other words, Prime members get on what we within the subscription industry call the 'golden handcuffs'; benefits for subscribers. As a result, Prime members end up spending three times as much money as non-members on Amazon.com in addition to the subscription fee.

- Prime is not just important to Amazon's current business, whereof a third of Amazon's turnover in the US derives from Prime memberships. Prime is also an important part of Amazon's strategy for the future that revolves around a complete disruption of the interplay between e-commerce and retail and a domination of the same-day delivery market.

- To win the position as the same-day delivery dominator in the market, Amazon has entered the market for groceries in the US. AmazonFresh delivers groceries and other goods directly to the customer's door step on the same day as the goods are ordered. Prime plays an important role here, too. A PrimeFresh subscription, at an annual sum of 299 USD, gives the customers free delivery of groceries as frequent as they like.

- Other retail and grocery businesses have much to learn from Amazon's subscription success. Businesses have the opportunity to tie customers closer to the business through a subscription that creates loyalty and makes the customer spend more with your business and less with the competitors.

- There is a great chance that we will see a substantial usage of the subscription model within both the retail market and the grocery market – just as we have seen it in other industries the last couple of years.

2 INTRODUCTION: AMAZON PRIME – THE WORLD'S MOST SUCCESSFUL SUBSCRIPTION BUSINESS?

Amazon is one of the world's biggest and also, without any doubt, one of the world's leading retailers. Also, Amazon remains ahead in the e-commerce market in the US and in the rest of the world. In 2015, Amazon's turnover reached a total of 107,01 billion USD, and Amazon now has a current value of 360 billion USD. Further, the growth rate is not looking like it is about to stop.

Amazon.com aired in the summer of 1995, and since then Amazon has managed to turn its business from being a digital bookstore into being an Internet-based product giant.

Today, it is almost impossible to find any items that Amazon *does not* sell. This and more, has brought an extraordinary growth and in 2013 Amazon was believed to be bigger than the closest nine competitors combined.

The reasons why Amazon is growing so rapidly has been discussed quite extensively. Two of the most important reasons is certainly Amazon's ability to think out of the box in relation to customers and industries and to reinvest its money. Moreover, the company's ability to think strategically, innovatively and farsighted at the same time holds importance. These abilities are all rooted in CEO and founder of Amazon, Jeff Bezos' way of thinking, but also shared by many of Amazon's current employees. Amazon Prime is one of these innovative and visionary thoughts that became action. Launched as a loyalty program in 2005, Amazon Prime has made it both easier and cheaper to be a customer at Amazon. In a relatively short time, Amazon Prime changed Amazon from being a traditional transaction-based e-commerce business to a unique and successful subscription business.

Along with exponential growth comes expansion of the range of competitors, which was also observed by Business Insider in 2014:

"As Amazon expands into more verticals, its sheer number of competitors has exploded, and they're attacking Amazon in ways that are both

big and small. Amazon remains a strong company, but it suddenly seems at risk of stretching itself too thin, exposing itself to too many competitors".

Even though this is a two-year-old observation, it is still valid. In 2016, Amazon is still in direct competition with those U.S online retailers identified in 2013. Adding to competitors are video-streaming services such as HBO and Hulu, and "cloud storage" services such as Dropbox. Further, due to its entry into different markets, Amazon has become slightly vulnerable to competitors such as app-based e-commerce start-ups, and challengers such as Google and Uber. Nonetheless, Amazon currently maintains a leading position.

When Amazon Prime launched in 2005, it was introduced as an annual membership providing members paying 79 USD a year, free two-day delivery on more than 1 million of Amazon's different products. Now, 11 years later, a Prime membership costs 99 USD yearly or 10.99 USD monthly, but in return, the selection of products – still delivered with no cost – is now more than 15 million. In accordance, the Prime that we experience today contains far more benefits for customers than it did 11 years ago.

Amazon has never released the actual number of Prime members, which has ignited many speculations. At the end of 2013, Amazon hinted that the number was more than 20 million. Now, three years later Consumer Intelligence Research Partners' has estimated the number of Prime members to be around 63 million.

There is no doubt that the numbers of members will continue to grow. The last couple of years, Amazon has really focused on Prime and the evolution of Prime. Amazon has added more elements to Prime and has realised that the concept is not just a convenient service for its customers. Prime has become a key element in Amazon's strategy of changing the retail and groceries industry completely.

At the same time, customers love Prime to such an extent that Amazon Prime – and hereby Amazon – is becoming the most successful subscription business in the world. This report is looking closer into facts, strategy and perspectives behind Amazon Prime. The report also takes a look at what other companies might learn from the success of Amazon.

3 BEHIND PRIME

11 years ago, in February 2005, the charismatic CEO Jeff Bezos announced that Amazon would release a new and revolutionary concept. The concept was Amazon Prime, a year-based membership that would give subscribers – regular Amazon users – free two-day delivery in exchange for an annual payment. Prior to this announcement, a hectic development process took place, which was driven by Jeff Bezos himself, who understood the enormous value that could lie in lowering the purchase barrier for loyal customers, and thus making them more loyal.

However, Jeff Bezos' project did not gain much internal acceptance in the beginning. On the face of it, it seemed like an unprofitable undertaking. If new Prime members did not purchase from Amazon more than 10 times a year, Amazon would lose money on its customers. Many within the company, therefore, feared that Prime would turn into a big money monster and become a millstone around the neck of the business. Nonetheless, Jeff Bezos stood his ground, and the concerns proved unfounded.

During the next six years Amazon Prime remained faithful to the original concept, which was to be a simple delivery system for loyal customers. But then Prime developed in new directions. In 2011, Prime expanded with a movie service. Further, Amazon Prime continued its development to be the service that we know today, also containing a music service, e-books, a photo storage service, a specialised service for families and much more. In 2016

Prime costs 99 USD a year or 10.99 a month and is available in the following countries besides the US: Germany, Japan, England, France, Italy, Spain, Austria and Canada.

As mentioned in the introduction, the number of Prime members is unknown, and even though Amazon has been intensely secretive about this, it seems as if speculations will never end. In 2015 the estimation was that Amazon Prime had 60 million subscribers, such as assessed by the Business Insider, which is very close to Consumer Intelligence Research Partners' estimation of 63 million Prime members in July 2016.

4 BEHIND THE SUCCESS – THE 'GOLDEN HANDCUFFS'; BENEFITS FOR SUBSCRIBERS

The fundamental element behind Amazon Prime's success is that users of Prime simply spend more money once they have become members of Prime. Analysts have calculated that Prime subscribers spend up to three times as much money at Amazon compared to regular customers. So far, it has seemed as if the increase in turnover quickly equalises Amazon's extra costs on delivery and additional services. Once the Prime subscriber has experienced the benefits of free delivery – and is already in the process of purchasing from Amazon – the temptation to shop elsewhere is suddenly diminished. Furthermore, the subscriber can be tempted to buy even more products, as most will have a need to recoup the yearly lump sum.

That it actually is so is no surprise to folks at Amazon. Already at the launch of Prime, Jeff Bezos had a clear feeling that Prime could help change the behaviour of customers and make them more loyal. With one-click orders, Amazon had already shown that you can remove a source of irritation when buying online, and make it easier and more simple to shop. This increase customers' motivation to buy, and the likelihood for them to return more often. Jeff Bezos predicted that the same thing would happen with Prime when they removed another source of irritation; the payment for delivery.

Robbie Schwietzer, head of Amazon Prime, has in fact said it even more to the point. Even though this quote is from the days where Prime was 20 USD cheaper than today the same mechanisms are in play:

"Once you become a Prime member, your human nature takes over. You want to leverage your $79 as much as possible. Not only do you buy more, but you buy in a broader set of categories. You discover all the selections we have that you otherwise wouldn't have thought to look to Amazon for". – Robbie Schwietzer, VP Amazon Prime

In other words, Prime members get on what might be called the 'golden handcuffs'; benefits for subscribers, a phenomenon that is also know from other subscription businesses. The customer is more loyal to the company where the subscription is purchased, because he or she feels that once the subscription is paid for, it becomes about getting as much as possible from the already paid subscription. This causes the subscriber to turn even more to the company and familiarise him- or herself less with competitors.

Thus, Prime has proved to be a powerful tool in building a strong relationship between Amazon and its customers. A relationship that has resulted in increased loyalty, more purchases and higher revenue per customer. But Prime is not only a means to lift the current business.

Prime is also a very important component in Amazon's future strategy concerning changing the retail and grocery market in the world. We will get back to that later in this report.

5 PRIME IN NUMBERS

A customer, who is a member of Prime, spends, as mentioned earlier, three times as much money with Amazon as a regular Amazon customer. More precisely, market research shows, based on US data, that a Prime member spends about 1,500 USD yearly from Amazon compared with 625 USD used by customers that are not Prime members. Also, the number of Prime memberships rose by 53 percent in 2014, despite the change in yearly subscription price from 79 USD to 99 USD.

Nevertheless, the recent initiative to make it possible for Prime members to pay a monthly subscription fee of 10.99 USD and to make Amazon Prime video streaming available to all Amazon users for 8.99 USD a month has generated some speculations on whether the annual subscription fee will increase. These speculations arise from breaking down the new monthly subscription fees over the course of a year. If you add them up to a 12-month subscription payment they reach a full year payment of 131.88 USD for the Prime membership and 107.88 USD for the Prime video membership. Only time will tell if Amazon has any intensions to raise prices, however, to exceed the psychological 100 USD barrier would seem as a big step to take.

One of the essential objectives of Prime is obviously to create value for Amazon, but it is unquestionably not difficult to understand that the service is also quite valuable for the consumer. Looking at the competition, you can easily pay 99 USD for just one of the alternatives that Amazon offers. With Prime you get all together in one package, which among other products and services includes Prime Music, Amazon's music streaming service, Prime Instant video, a video streaming service, and Amazon Cloud Drive, Amazon's "cloud storage". For example, Netflix costs 96 USD per year, Spotify Premium costs 120 USD per year, and Dropbox, with associated 1 terabyte data also costs 120 USD per year.

Yet, it is not even in the bundling aspect that the consumer saves the most money. If you analyse it, consumers can save most money on the delivery. A standard delivery with UPS (United Postal Service) costs between 10 and 15 USD for a normal package. One does not have to order more than ten packages a year before it becomes a good business, and there are many examples of users that have ordered even more packages than that. New York Times has written about a user with 90 orders at Amazon over the past year – that amount would approximately round up to a total of 1,000 USD just for delivery. You can clearly see a consumer pattern; Prime is worth the money for the subscriber.

But as mentioned earlier, it has to be profitable for both parties before it turns into a good business. There is no doubt that the actual delivery cost is not profitable for Amazon, but that does not seem to be important, if you get the customer to spend more money when the customer is at your site. Besides, Amazon obviously earn money on the actual subscription fees: If Amazon Prime has 50 million users – and we assume that about 10 million of those are on a trial basis or other special basis – Amazon roughly earns 4 billion USD just on the subscription payment. According to analysts, around one third of Amazon's US turnover today is from Prime in the form of subscription revenue and in terms of the products Prime members buy.

6 THE DEVELOPMENT OF PRIME

Amazon Prime began as a service that offered its customers free two-day delivery. Since then, Prime has been continuously developed and expanded, and today the service is much more than just free delivery. Here is a review of the developments of Prime and the services that are available today:

6.1 FREE TWO-DAY DELIVERY

This was where it all started. For six years, Prime was solely a free two-day delivery service, and it was, for the subscribers, a genuine success. It was possible to get free delivery with your purchase, if you ordered for more than 25 USD and was not a Prime subscriber, but as Prime subscriber you could order anything you wanted without paying for the transportation. Of course, you indirectly paid for the load – in the form of the yearly payment – but at the end most customers saved more on the free transport than he or she paid in the subscription sum.

Actually, it was rather clear that Amazon was losing money in the beginning. From the beginning, it was far from being a money machine. It was more important for Jeff Bezos to build customer loyalty. Bezos and his team knew from past experience that such an initiative would change how customers behaved and motivate them to yield even larger orders. Prime customers were, as Jeff Bezos predicted, loving the free delivery service and, therefore ordered indiscriminately; more, bigger and different goods than previously predicted. The fundament for Prime was born, and today the free two-day delivery service has extended to more than 15 million items. The free delivery service remains a cornerstone of Prime for most members.

Amazon also participates in the collaborative consumption wave. As a customer, it is possible to share your membership. Prime subscribers can share their free two-day delivery service with up to four members of the family or with their workplace. However, it is only the delivery that can be shared – not music, movies or other Prime goods.

If Amazon misses the scheduled delivery date for Prime subscribers, the subscriber can, as a compensation, look forward to a one-month free extension of their Prime subscription.

6.2 PRIME INSTANT VIDEO

The video service competes with some relatively big players including Netflix, Hulu and HBO. Nonetheless there are many indications towards that Prime Instant Video is a huge success, especially with reference to getting users to subscribe to Prime or getting users to continue to stay with Prime.

The video service is quite simple containing a large selection of available movies and series, as we know it from Netflix. Amazon has even added self-produced TV series, like *Bosch*, to its assortment, and it does not seem as if the development and the competition with the big players is over – Amazon has only just begun to challenge this segment.

As for the video service's importance in relation to the rest of the service, some studies show that members, who watch videos on the streaming service, renew their membership far more often than those who do not use the video service, and that those who use the streaming service during their 30-day trial period are more likely to convert to the full version of Prime.

Recently, Amazon Prime video has become available to all Amazon users, as a standalone option for 8.99 USD a month after a 30-day free trial. In this way, Amazon directly challenges competitors like Netflix, who offers its standard service for 9.99 USD a month.

6.3 AMAZON STUDIOS

Amazon Studios is an additional step in Amazon's long-term plan to reach as many users as possible. Amazon Studios is Amazon's own film production service and intends to produce both TV series and movies. Currently, it has only produced television series, but up to several films have been announced and scheduled. Amazon is trying to involve its users in Studios by giving them the opportunity to come up with the next *House of Cards* or *Game of Thrones*. At Studios, it is possible to submit one's project or idea and at best to get it produced. Here we are of course talking about extreme cases, as the service is not an amateur service. But the concept itself and that the opportunity is there, make the user know that

Amazon finds it important to involve its users in its operations.

As a Prime-subscriber there are of course some advantages, besides having access to the streaming service. Early access to specific television series (and probably movies when they come) is available to the subscriber, as well as ideas, tests, and other things in connection to the film will also be available for the subscriber to a certain extent.

6.4 PRIME MUSIC

Prime Music is Amazon's music streaming service. Here users get access to over a million songs that can be freely downloaded to a "Prime-Library". Prime users also have the opportunity to buy a CD at a lower price than usual, even if these purchases are rare in these times.

Compared with Spotify and other music services, Prime Music's selection is not ostentatious, as the competitors have over 20 million songs available, but simply that the selection exists is incredibly important and gives the loyal customers good value for their money. The service is a strong sign from Amazon to its customers about constantly wanting to be where the consumers are, and that it strives to make Prime more than just "worth the money".

Due to the recent initiative of making Prime Video a separate service, it now seems more likely that Prime Music, in the future, could bring new competition to Spotify and Apple Music.

6.5 AMAZON CLOUD DRIVE

Amazon Cloud Drive is Amazon's "cloud storage"; Amazon's response to Dropbox. Here, users can store files from their computers so that it has a backup and so that the computer's own memory does not get filled up.

In addition, as a Prime user one gets just that extra thing – you get an unlimited photo storage with Amazon Prime Photos. This photo storage service was added to Prime in 2014, and the service gives Prime users a direct backup of their images on their phones, which is also unlimited, and which reportedly receives the vast majority of image files. The photo storage gives all users of Amazon Prime a sensible reason not to use Dropbox, and in this way, increases its own lever on the different customer segments.

6.6 AMAZON MOM

Amazon Mom is a further membership in Prime. As a Prime subscriber, it is possible to subscribe as either a parent or a family member, and in this way, save 15–20 percent on diapers and similar products. However, the name has been in a bit of a limelight and has therefore been changed to the more appropriate "Amazon Family".

6.7 SIX MONTHS OF FREE MEMBERSHIP FOR STUDENTS

Many of tomorrow's customers are currently students. They come into the market with knowledge of digital services, they are known as very convenience-seeking, and they have a relatively great willingness to buy. But most importantly, an early influence on these people can create long relationships with a solid amount of trust and consequently a huge potential customer segment.

Prime Student is an offer to all students in higher education in either the UK or the US, which includes a six-month free Prime membership. This means that young people have the opportunity to enjoy the service of free delivery for half a year. As one can shop both books and clothes at the same place, there is no doubt that the convenience of Prime is very attractive to young buyers.

6.8 KINDLE AND PRIME LIBRARY

39 percent of Amazon's consumers in the US allegedly own a Kindle reader. Kindle users who are not necessarily Prime subscribers, are often mentioned as just as good customers as Prime subscribers, because they tend to purchase more than the "standard" customer.

Kindle is the name of Amazon's e-book reader, which gives users the possibility to purchase, download and read e-books on their tablet anytime. The Kindle also works in conjunction with Prime Library, which gives Prime subscribers the possibility to borrow e-books for free from the website or the app.

6.9 PRIME NOW

Prime Now is a relatively new concept from Amazon that comes from the idea of fast delivery – Prime Now just has to be even faster. In 2014 the idea of delivery within an hour in the Manhattan area of New York was launched. The goal was that the concept should be implemented in several cities during 2015. It is now available in cities such as Atlanta, Chicago, Dallas, Las Vegas, Miami, Orlando, Phoenix, Portland, Sacramento, San Francisco Bay Area, Virginia Beach and more. The concept is very simple: For 7.99 USD, Prime subscribers can receive supplies of certain goods on the doorstep within one hour.

If it takes two hours, the delivery is free. This gives Amazon a brand-new opportunity to challenge the traditional shopping patterns, as it is usually the time used to go to the supermarket and back again – now most Prime members can save that time for something different. This gives the subscriber an excess of time and more freedom.

6.10 PRIME FREE – SAME-DAY DELIVERY

According to a report from Business Insider, it has been expected that the market for same-day delivery in the US would explode in the coming years. Unsurprisingly, Amazon has beaten this speculation to the punch by already implementing a free same-day delivery for Prime members in eligible zip codes in the US.

The "Holy Grail" in e-commerce is same-day delivery – that is, when the goods are delivered to the consumer the same day that he or she ordered them, and often within a few hours after ordering. Therefore, the biggest change in the relationship between e-commerce and physical stores has been expected to happen, when the time that passes from the customer orders a product until it is delivered is so short that it is not worthwhile for the consumer to pick up the product himself or herself. Amazon is currently contributing to this change.

6.11 AMAZON PRIME AIR

Amazon Prime Air is not a finished concept…yet! It's all about air delivery via drones, and it is something that Amazon and Jeff Bezos have looked forward to in a while now. The project seems viable, since 86 percent of Amazon's parcels actually weigh less than a drone can carry. For Amazon, it would provide an opportunity to economise the person delivering the packages. For the subscriber, it would not just be a great experience to have your package delivered through the air, but in the long run it would probably also be the fastest delivery.

6.12 PRIME DAY

Last year Amazon Prime launched a rival to Black Friday – its one-day sale event Prime Day, which is meant to reward Prime subscribers with exclusive deals ranging from deals on electronics, such as tablets, TV and laptops to clothing, shoes, jewellery, kitchenware and so on. Amazon Prime Day 2016 was supposedly the 'biggest day in the history of Amazon'.

According to Techradar, "Amazon says it shipped 60 percent more products worldwide compared to Prime Day 2015, with a 50 percent boost in its home territory of the US."

Obvious to most, Prime Day is yet another success of Amazon.

6.13 AMAZON DASH BUTTON

The Dash Button is one of the most recent initiatives launched by Amazon, which is a Wi-Fi connected button that, when pressed, instantly purchases or reorders a product from Amazon. The Dash Button is linked to a product of your choice, so that when you are running low on products, such as washing powder for your washing machine, toilet paper, dishwashing tablets, coffee, hand lotion, diapers or the like, you simply press the button.

Amazon will, thereafter, deliver the products to your doorstep, just as with any other Amazon Prime delivery. Essentially, this service is exclusively for Prime members, and seems as another attempt for Amazon to handcuff its members into its Prime subscription service.

The Dash Button costs 4.99 USD, which is the same price that members will receive as credit after their first press on the button. Amazon first launched the Dash button in the US last year in march, and has been available in three other countries outside the US: The U.K., Germany, and Austria. This service is about ultimate convenience for consumers, who can choose between more than 40 brands, such as Air Wick, Ariel, Dettol, Vanish, Gillette, and Nescafé. Moreover, the Dash Button is also an opportunity for brands, such as Siemens, Boss and Whirlpool to increase in sales. This is seen as a possibility for these brands to produce dishwashers and washing machines with a Dash Replenishment Service (DRS) integration for ordering dishwasher tablets or detergent automatically.

7 THE LONG-TERM STRATEGY BEHIND PRIME

Even though the current Prime program appears to be a huge success for Amazon, the company is far from finished with developing and transforming the future of the retail industry in the US and around the world. Jeff Bezos and his colleagues at Amazon are known to have visions of the future to such a degree that it can take your breath away.

Actually, Bezos does not disregard any chance to tell both employees and the outside world that Amazon is still in "Day One" in relation to the development of both the Internet and the company itself. Bezos is also wearing the long-term glasses in terms of Prime and its further development. The development of Prime, as we know it today, is just the first step in a strategic plan that aims to fundamentally change the relationship between e commerce and physical stores.

The second step in Amazon's strategy is and has been an expansion of the already large and complicated machine of logistics. In the US, Amazon already has more than 100 large fulfilment centres, i.e. huge warehouses and distribution centres from where Amazon can reach all major populated areas in the US within a few hours' drive. Outside the US, Amazon has more than 50 fulfilment centres, mainly in Europe. The plan is that these distribution centres should operate the majority of Amazon's customers with a same-day delivery service.

Therefore, the final step in the strategic plan's three-stage rocket is to ensure that Amazon's customers increasingly ask for same-day delivery. This will be done via Amazon's entry into the market for groceries. The mean to achieve this strategic goal is called AmazonFresh.

8 AMAZONFRESH AND PRIMEFRESH

AmazonFresh is a service that delivers groceries – and other items – directly to the customers' doorstep the same day as the goods are ordered or the following morning. AmazonFresh started as a service for customers in the Seattle area. Today an assortment of about 100,000 items are offered in certain postcodes in the US, among which cities such as Los Angeles, San Francisco, San Diego, New York and Philadelphia are included. The plan is to continue to roll out AmazonFresh in new cities both within and outside the US.

With the expansion of AmazonFresh, Amazon has also involved the popular and successful Prime program. As a customer of AmazonFresh you can buy a PrimeFresh membership for 299 USD per year, which gives access to free delivery of all grocery purchases from AmazonFresh – besides all the other benefits that Prime offers its members. The goal of

PrimeFresh is of course the obvious: To get customers who are used to buy once or twice a month to buy once or twice a week or, if possible, even more often.

The mission appears to succeed, because just as with Prime, Amazon is experiencing that members of AmazonFresh are not only buying more, but also more often than non-members, just as PrimeFresh members purchase more than the regular Prime members. Thus, all the same purchase mechanisms as with Prime members also apply for PrimeFresh members.

Once customers have bought their membership, then they want to get the most out of it. Consequently, members shop more and more at Amazon than they would have done otherwise. The flywheel of positivity for Amazon is set in motion.

9 CONCLUSION: WHAT CAN OTHERS LEARN FROM AMAZON?

In 20 years Amazon, has managed to grow from nothing to the world's most successful e-commerce company with an annual turnover of over 100 billion USD and a market value of around 360 billion USD. Yet, the company still finds itself in "Day One" in the development of e-commerce, because the vast majority of trade between companies and individuals is still physical and done by customers psychically going into a store or a supermarket. This is what Amazon wants to change.

According to Jeff Bezos and Amazon that change will only happen if e-commerce in the future is both cheaper, faster and easier for the customer than it is for the customer to go down to the local store or supermarket. Therefore, the customer, when he or she is purchasing online, must have access to the best and largest selection of items. More importantly, the goods need to be delivered quickly and most often the very same day.

One of the most surprising levers that Amazon has done in the creation of this change has been to turn its customers into to subscribers. The subscription model is otherwise not an everyday sight in the retail or grocery industry. In fact, it is virtually non-existent, but Amazon has reinvented and revolutionized the concept of subscription and have created a very strong formula for customer loyalty with Amazon Prime. In fact, to such an extent that it is assumed that Amazon has more than 60 million subscribers worldwide – and still rising!

Why is it that Prime is such a success for Amazon? There are two very important reasons.

Firstly, Prime makes it much easier for customers to shop online, while removing one of the major barriers in e-commerce: Payment for delivery. This lowers the purchase barrier for the customer, who then rewards Amazon with multiple purchases. Secondly, Amazon uses "bundling" as a key strategy by adding more and more services and more and more content to Prime. Besides delivery, members also have access to music, movies, data storage, and much more as part of the subscription. It is no coincidence that the number of Prime members has grown explosively in recent years, where total services of Prime has also risen.

Amazon uses a very deliberate strategy that concerns tying members even closer to the services and providing customers with an experience of value-for-money. Once the many services are being used, it is much harder for the customer to leave the services again. For example, research shows that new Amazon Prime members, who use video service in their free trial period converts in higher rate than those who do not use this part of the service.

So the many built-in services help both in terms of new sales, conversion and retention.

It's funny to think of how Prime started as a coincidence. In fact, it was an idea that was submitted in one of Amazon's Idea Boxes as a staff proposal. A proposal that, for a long time, was regarded with great scepticism at Amazon. Today Prime is an important cornerstone of the company in relation to current earnings and in relation to the future strategy. A strategy in which Amazon's next move will be a strong entry into the market for groceries in the US and worldwide.

The question is what other retail- and grocery businesses can learn from Amazon?

It is obvious that almost everyone can learn from Amazon's way of doing e-commerce business – an extensive number of books have been written about that. Amazon has really set the stage, and today there is hardly no retail and/or grocery business that does not have a strategy for how to access the e-commerce market, and for how the physical and the digital store should work together. At the same time, most of the large retail companies have a plan for how to become resistant to competition from precisely Amazon.

This applies extensively in the US and to a lesser degree in Europe, where Amazon is present without being quite as dominant as at its place of origin.

By and large all retail and grocery businesses can learn from Amazon's way of running a subscription business, though it is not that acknowledged. In fact, the authors claim that only very few retail- and grocery businesses have strategies or plans for how they can run their business as a subscription business. It may seem strange due to the great success that Amazon has had with Prime, but in a way, Amazon has managed to keep the success under the radar for many people.

It is quite obvious that the subscription model has a great potential to create loyal customers who buy more and more, where they are members, and less and less from competitors.

Who would not want customers to subscribe to one's store?

Just as Amazon have revolutionised the retail industry in relation to e-commerce, Amazon Prime will in the same way revolutionise the grocery industry in relation to thinking in subscriptions and memberships.

10 ABOUT SUBSCRYBE

Subscrybe was founded in the summer of 2011 with a mission to support the subscription revolution and make the subscription model the preferred business model for both consumers and businesses. This is done by creating Europe's leading company within innovation and development of subscription-based businesses.

Subscrybe collaborates with existing subscription companies to develop their businesses and improve all subscription processes – sales to new customers, retention of existing customers, and win-back of former customers. We are also working on developing new subscription strategies and shaping the subscription products of the future.

Furthermore, Subscrybe works on developing new subscription businesses in collaboration with companies that do not yet use the subscription model.

www.ingramcontent.com/pod-product-compliance
Lightning Source LLC
Chambersburg PA
CBHW030058230526
45471CB00003B/1145